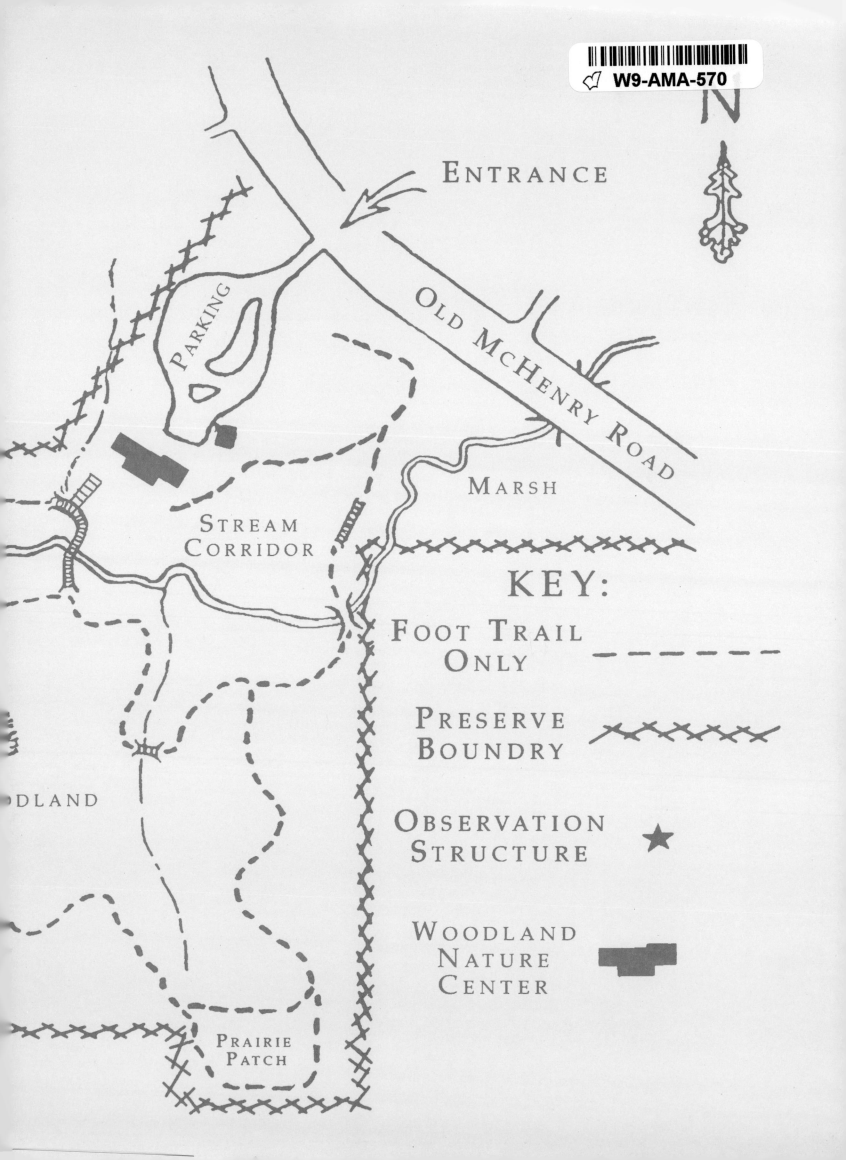

ENTRANCE

N

OLD McHENRY ROAD

PARKING

MARSH

STREAM
CORRIDOR

KEY:

FOOT TRAIL
ONLY

PRESERVE
BOUNDRY

OBSERVATION
STRUCTURE

★

WOODLAND
NATURE
CENTER

WOODLAND

PRAIRIE
PATCH

36
Acres

In 1933, photographer Charles Cook wrote
to thank Guy Reed for the use of his land (what
would become the Reed-Turner Nature Preserve)
as a setting for his portraits of nudes. In his note,
Mr. Cook described the property as....

"The most poetic piece of woodland I have
ever seen. For over ten years its enchantment and
beauty has always lured me back."

Through the foresight of Guy Reed and his
daughter, Barbara, little has changed and much
has been preserved.

36 ACRES

A Portrait of the Reed-Turner Woodland Nature Preserve

By

Tobin Fraley

Woodland Grove Press

This book is for:

Barbara Turner

A tireless environmentalist and teacher whose knowledge, wisdom and kindness have been and continue to be an inspiration to hundreds of people. Without her encouragement and friendship, this book would not exist.

ACKNOWLEDGEMENTS
As with any project, the sum of the whole is equal to its parts. There are many people who have been instrumental in the completion of this book and whose suggestions, thoughts, critiques and support have made working on this book a true joy. First of all, I thank my wife, Rachel Perkal, for her love and understanding over the last seven years of my running off into the woods with camera in hand. Also, my photography guru, Bill Kane; our Sunday evening writing group, Meredith Barber, Jim Christle, Elisa Karbin, Jacob Shaw, Jerry King, Mallery Lutey, Melissa MacTaggert and Maria Viktoria Abricka; Linda Tiffany and David Solnit for their encouragement and proof reading; my very good friend, Tori Trauscht; Dick Schuettge, my friend and mentor who could convince Diogenes to put down his lamp; my parents, Maurice and Nina Fraley; my wonderful sister Jenny Juelich and her equally wonderful husband Sputnik Juelich; and my cheering section of Eve Perkal, Karen Zukor & Paul Salinger, Bob & Mandy Schnack, Erin Johnson, Karen Schmitt, Karen Krahn, and Marna Spence.

Printed - April, 2010

Text and Photography
Copyright © 2010 by Tobin Fraley

www.36acres.com

Published by
Woodland Grove Press
3612 Rolling Glen Drive
Long Grove, IL 60047

ISBN: 978-0-913751-85-5

A portion of the proceeds from the sale of this book go to the Reed-Turner Woodland Trust for the continuing restoration, preservation and maintenance of the Reed-Turner Woodland Nature Preserve.

The Reed-Turner Woodland Trust and the Long Grove Park District are not responsible for the content of this book.

Library of Congress Cataloguing-in-Publication Data available.

Book Design by Tobin Fraley. Typefaces - Palatino Roman throughout except Papyrus used for Quotes. Printed on acid-free paper with greater than 50% recycled content.

Printed in Korea
through Overseas Printing Corp.
San Francisco, CA
www.overseasprinting.com

Contents ⚜

FOREWORD

by Tori Trauscht

My love affair with Reed-Turner Woodland began in 1999 when I was walking on the snowy trails with a friend. I had never visited before, but I recall it as a beautiful January day. As we walked we were enthralled by the quiet snow flakes that fell gently around us and the sound of the water as it trickled through the frozen stream. Since then I have come to know the place much more intimately. The following year, I began to work closely with the woodland's steward and founder, Barbara Reed Turner, to help restore the stream corridor and some of the other special habitats in this hidden sanctuary. In the past eight years I have become captivated by these 36 acres of wonder.

The rich history of this place is apparent as you walk nearly a mile along its hillside paths. The central ravines are in the eastern part of the Valparaiso Moraine that was originally carved out by receding glaciers nearly ten thousand years ago. This moraine now separates the valleys between the Upper Des Plaines and the Fox River systems in northeastern Illinois. The south branch of Indian Creek, also know as Kildeer Creek, flows through this portion of southern Lake County bordered by a wide section of ample floodplain for the rising waters that engulf the stream corridor several times a year. This "long grove" region is part of the Chicago area's oak-hickory forests that was one of a number of forest pockets

Bird Watchers at Reed Turner

originally surrounded by seas of prairie grasslands. Old McHenry Road, on the east, was an Indian trail, a route probably used by French traders, that later became a major thoroughfare for settlers who traversed the Long Grove area in the early 1800's and settled here in the 1840's.

Reed Pond and Salem Lake, border the southwest section of the site. These are two portions of a man-made lake that were created around the 1930's. Reed Pond was made by damming an area of a former marsh near where the Guy Reed family established a country home. Guy and Florence, Barbara's parents, then built their permanent home here in 1937. Once Barbara married Harold Turner, they lived in the cabin (which is now the nature center) and raised their family there until about 1975.

In 1959 Barbara began taking classes at the Morton Arboretum. The renowned naturalist and writer, May Watts was one of her instructors. She taught her the true value of the high quality land and woodlands still intact here and some of her classes visited the woodland. In the 1970's Barbara and her family decided to work with land agencies to preserve the land for perpetuity. They were raised to appreciate what they had, share what they could, and since selling such high quality land for development was not a consideration they decided to make it a preserve in memory of her parents. The woodland was given by the Turners to the Illinois Chapter of The Nature Conservancy. Several years later it was transferred to the Long Grove Park District and endowed with a trust fund that was established with grant funding. Because of its high quality and diversity it was dedicated an Illinois State Nature Preserve in the 1980's, one of the highest protections land can attain in the state.

Spraying for invasives

There are several ecosystem habitats that make up Reed-Turner Woodland. These generally include upland and lowland oak woodland and more open oak savanna communities, a ridge of maple woods, wet bottomland woods, prairies, wetland floodplain and marsh. Understory shrubs are present in some areas but conspicuously absent in others because of heavy deer browsing and the historic clearing of invasive buckthorn over the past 50 years. Hazelnut was present here at the time of the 1838 original land survey which shows settlement of the land, but the shrubs disappeared with lack of fire management and increased human and deer populations. Reed-Turner Woodland was one of the first locations in Illinois to begin a pilot program of prescribed fire burns of the woodlands in the early 1980's. Stewards Barbara Turner and John Clemetsen, Lee Bassett, and countless other valuable volunteers and friends have helped restore the woodland to what it is today.

I began working at the woodland as a volunteer on my first grant under the Indian Creek Watershed Project. Our volunteer board had chosen the site for restoration in 2000 since it is one of the highest quality areas in the Indian Creek watershed. We chose the historic sedge meadow as the restoration component for our Illinois Environmental Protection Agency Section 319 grant, a "clean water act" grant to prevent indirect pollution and educate people about the value of watersheds. The old sedge meadow had become overgrown with weedy, shade promoting trees, greatly declining since it had been a blooming wetland meadow where horses grazed in the 1940's (as Barbara recounted from her childhood). The years of grazing, excessive shade, and lack of understory native plants had caused erosion problems where soils would regularly wash through the flood-prone stream systems.

So the Reed-Turner Woodland stewards, our Indian Creek board members, volunteers and hired contractors, cut out 60 or 70 lesser trees that had moved in (ash, cherry, walnut, basswood) and this gradually lightened the canopy. We then replanted the floodplain corridor with a careful mix of native plants and seed. Over several years we managed the site for invasive species until the native plants had taken hold and erosion problems were finally eliminated. The "daylighting" of the corridor helped struggling native sedges to re-emerge and thrive after many years of darkened conditions.

During my subsequent employment with the Long Grove Park District I worked on 10 more grants to restore upland areas at the woodland and other park district sites. With our work and the careful dedication of hundreds of volunteers before us, this unique place has become a fully restored woodland complex. Important, regular prescribed burning has restored the woodland to its current glory and it has become a haven for many rare plants and creatures. Many scientific projects have taken place at the woodland, including burn studies, bird counts, plant audits, soil studies, tree, amphibian and habitat assessments, to name a few. The woodland has been carefully managed by Barbara and her many supporters over the years. If you walk the site on a day in late April, when all the woodland wildflowers are in bloom, you will understand the difference this kind of care can achieve.

Each day I spend at the Reed-Turner Woodland has gradually caused this place to become a part of me, through my hands and my heart as I pull another noxious garlic mustard plant, help during a prescribed burn, breathe the precious forest air, or as I hear the wind sigh across Salem Lake at sunset. I am lucky to have happened upon this place. I met Tobin on a trail here and learned new skills when I participated in his Chicago Botanic Garden sponsored photography class a few years ago. Tobin, Barbara, Jane Wittig, and many other supporters of habitat preservation are fiercely protective of this special place. Thankfully, there are many other special wild acres like this in the Chicago region, and groups like Chicago Wilderness where people have dedicated their lives to preserving these worthy remnants of natural history.

We are fortunate that we still have these places in Chicago… lands with rare trees and plants, lands that give gifts to us everyday in their colors, blooms, the rare insects and other creatures who find their refuge there. This book demonstrates the gift of refuge we have received from this type of land ethic that allows us to glimpse our rich historic past, through our preserved land. If you have been here you know what Reed-Turner Woodland has to give and it may call you back, but when you visit here, please tread lightly, stay on the path and take only pictures. This is one of those sacred spaces we must preserve for future generations so that it can flourish

Barbara Turner and John Clemetsen working on a controlled burn in the Reed-Turner Woodland

for generations. When you get to know the woodland as I have, it will grow into you as well. Whether it's the humming of the dragonflies on a summer day, the sight of twin fawns as they hide quietly in the underbrush, or a painter's pallet of tree and grass colors as they change hue in the fall, it becomes a part of us all.

I leave you with my favorite memory as you witness the woodland in these pages. Once, on a lazy afternoon, as I was walking the trails looking for dreaded patches of invasive garlic mustard to pull, the trail led me to the stream after quietly making my way downhill. All at once I came face to face with a beautiful coyote as he also quietly canvassed the stream corridor. I remember we were separated by the narrow water, only about ten feet apart, as our eyes locked for just a second or two. I was in awe of his extraordinary tawny coat and healthy appearance. Then, in a flash, he turned and darted off at what seemed 60 miles per hour. This was my moment, my special encounter with the wildness of this place … if you are quiet you never know what you too may experience here. I am honored I was asked to write the forword of "36 Acres." Here Tobin Fraley has provided you your own private journey of fleeting visions of this lovely and rare Illinois gem. Enjoy the visit, bask in the beauty of the Reed-Turner Woodland, and help us protect it so it can keep surprising us!

Tori Trauscht
Founder and Director
Indian Creek Watershed Project

Introduction ᴡ

Across the split rail fence that surrounds our backyard sits the Reed-Turner Woodland Nature Preserve. Compared to other nature preserves, the thirty-six acres of the Reed-Turner Woodland is rather small. On any given morning, a brisk walk around the preserve may take as little as fifteen minutes. So it is easy to understand why it remains relatively unknown, even to many who live just down the road or around the corner.

Yet the size of this preserve gives new meaning to the old saying that great things come in small packages, for it was on a stroll in the spring of 2000 that I began to see the remarkable beauty and diversity of what my wife, Rachel, and I have come to view as an extension of our backyard. I soon began to explore the woodland with greater frequency, finding that each walk would reveal something new. Some days, it was the way light would filter through the trees. Sometimes it was a new wildflower that appeared overnight. And as the seasons changed, the newly fallen snow or a dense fog would dramatically alter the preserve, creating an entirely new place to discover.

In early January of 2003 I began recording the moods, the seasonal changes and the details of the woodland. As the snow started to fall that first day, I found my camera and, asking Rachel to come with me, we headed into the preserve. A few of the images taken that day are still among my favorites.

Since then I have taken thousands of photographs in the Reed-Turner Woodland. The original goal of capturing some aspects of the preserve has changed into a full-time project to create a comprehensive portrait of the woods, stream, and prairie in all its seasons, while documenting the myriad flowers, insects, animals, and trees that live in and frequent this small parcel of land.

In the process of this exploration I have had opportunities to photograph many other spectacular areas around this nation. In traveling around the country there is no doubt that the gorges of the Grand Canyon or the towers of Monument Valley are breathtaking. The splendors of our national parks are beyond words. But there are also times that we look for the extraordinary qualities of nature in the famous landmarks of this country while the beauty of our own backyard is taken for granted.

So as I delve deeper into the qualities of this nature preserve and as I continue to learn more about the art of photography, I have come to realize that there is not an end to this project. The more photographs I take, the more I see what I have not yet captured.

Tobin Fraley
Long Grove, IL
June 2008

In the attitude of silence the soul finds the
path in a clearer light, and what is elusive and
deceptive resolves itself into crystal clearness.
Our life is a long and arduous quest after Truth.

- Mahatma Gandhi -

A Portrait of the Reed-Turner Woodland Nature Preserve

Spring

And yet, as always, the springtime sun brings forth new life, and we may rejoice because of this new life and contribute to its unfolding.

- Albert Einstein -

EMERGING

Every February the plum trees that lined the streets of Berkeley would fill with pink blossoms and even though it was technically still winter, this was my sign that spring was on its way.

The seasons here in the Midwest are different. The plants that are prevalent in the summer months, become dormant with the cold and snow. Finally, when the ground begins to thaw and the days move towards the summer soltice, bits of green begin to appear. Despite the number of times I have seen this change of season, I am still amazed to find the first new growth pushing through the undergrowth and stretching towards the light.

By May a carpet of flora dots the meadows and hillsides. The leaves from fall still cover the ground, but they begin to fade into the background and soon the changes in the landscape become so rapid that each day offers a new version of the woodland.

HARBINGER

 As spring approaches, the signs are everywhere. A robin pulls worms from the newly thawed ground, the first green pokes through matted leaves or the last clump of icy snow melts away.

 Regardless of all of these markers, for me there is only one sure sign that I watch and listen for each day as winter exits. The moment the first Sandhill Cranes announce themselves, I know the warmth of spring cannot be far away.

 When I hear the far away chatter of that initial flock, I scan the sky knowing that the birds are nearby, but all I see are clouds and blue. As their calls increase, the sound begins to fill the air and I eventually pinpoint the tiny specks high above me.

 Even though there may be something lost in translation, at the moment those first Cranes pass overhead, what I hear them tell me is that at last spring has arrived.

WILDFLOWERS

No matter that it has happened all my life or that it has happened for millions of years in the past and that it will continue long after I am gone, I always enter spring in a state of nervous apprehension. *Will the wildflowers come back?*

Each day, in the first part of April, I search the woodland for signs of the delicate Hepatica. And although there is a great sense of relief when I finally spot the fuzzy young shoots, I then begin to fret about the Bloodroot, then the Trout Lilies, the Trillium and so on throughout the summer.

My anxiety does not bring them back year after year and certainly the wildflowers do not bloom for me, but I want to be a part of the process, to watch over and to protect them. So even though I know that worry will not make them reappear, perhaps a little concern is not such a bad thing.

People from a planet without flowers
would think we must be mad with joy
the whole time to have such things
about us.

~ Iris Murdoch ~

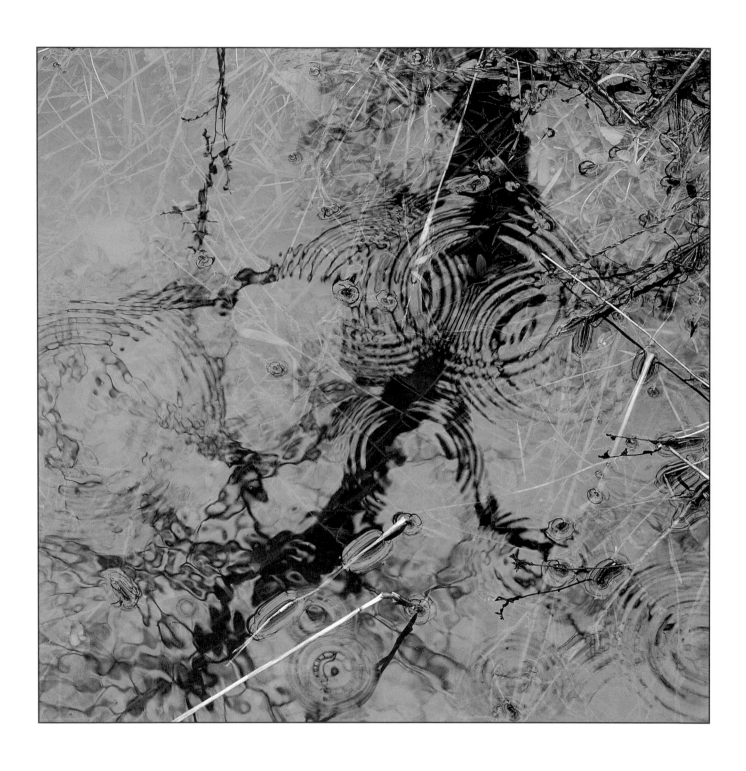

RAIN

Rain arrives in many forms. Sometimes a passing cloud that appears to contain no more than a trace of water will scatter a few large heavy drops across the dry landscape. At other times, dark thunderheads build in the sky and bear down upon the woodland, drenching the earth. More often the rain arrives in steady day-long showers that saturate the soil, filtering through the ground to the deep-rooted wildflowers and replenishing the aquifer.

On these days I stay inside and watch the rain coat the woods for there is something comforting about the sound of the water drumming against the roof's cedar shingles.

And then there is the morning after; when the plants have had their fill and the leaves shake off the leftover drops like a dog after an unwanted bath; when the forest glistens in the sun's light as if covered with a sugar glaze and the newly cleaned air smells of fresh moist earth.

Night

At the end of each day, the sunlight wanes and night covers the preserve, allowing the nocturnal creatures that roam the darkened woodland to emerge.

This is the time for owls and for the mice that rustle among the dry leaves and for the bullfrogs that bellow along the shoreline. This is the time for crickets to sing and for coyotes to howl, and now and then, for some unknown animal to let lose an unearthly cry that echoes through the underbrush.

This is also the time when the sky is cleared of the day's blue mask, freeing the stars and moon to drop their light through silhouetted branches and onto the forest floor. Except for these bits of starlight, the night remains unseen to me, for my eyes are not those of the fox whose vision can penetrate the darkness. And so I remain at the edge of the woodland, content just to listen to these sounds that move through the still, night air.

The Steward

Books offering photographs of nature rarely include images of people or even the evidence of human influence. Yet mankind is as much a part of nature as any animal, mountain stream or meadow of wildflowers. The regrettable reason for our exclusion is that, more often than not, the images available are ones of the damage we inflict upon the earth and the alteration of the environment in which we live and breathe.

Fortunately, within the many people who populate this planet, there are those whose "footprint" is not one of carbon but one of kindness, compassion, and a love of the earth that is combined with an unassuming, innate wisdom of life. Barbara Turner is just such a person.

She has guided the preservation and restoration of the land surrounding her childhood home with such gentle determination that she herself has become an integral part of the landscape. Barbara has left (and continues to leave) a very large footprint on the Reed-Turner Woodland, but it is an invisible footprint that can only be seen by closing your eyes and listening to the sounds of the woodland.

TERRITORY

On an early spring morning when a bit of winter cool still lingers in the air, I take a book and a sweater, place myself in a backyard chair and read. Occasionally I glance up and scan the preserve across the pond and now and then I notice someone walking along the path near the pond's edge. Without thinking, I react with a territorial imperative, wondering what this intruder is doing in "my" preserve.

When this scene played out again a few weeks ago, I went inside to find the binoculars in order to assess this trespasser's imagined threat. As I adjusted the focus onto a single person, a woman dressed in brown, she stopped for a moment along the path, tilted her head back and closed her eyes. I could feel the woodland wash over and through her.

I put down the binoculars and looked away. At that moment I ceded whatever sense of ownership I had over to her, even though I knew full well that the forest was never mine to give. Since that day, I use the binoculars for spotting birds and I leave those who have only come to walk the paths and revel in the peace of the woodland to themselves.

GREAT BLUE HERON

There is something prehistoric about herons. They circle Reed Pond like feathered pterodactyls that hang in the air, as if held up by translucent strings. Eventually they choose a spot to land and approach the pond with such precision that the water where they light barely ripples.

Except during winter months, these great birds are regular guests along the shoreline of the pond, sometimes perching on a nearby branch, as they survey their domain with a regal indifference. And even though I see these birds every day for much of the year, I never tire of watching them. Tall, lean and stealthy on the ground, majestic and graceful in the air, they remind me that despite the woes of the world, there are small pieces of life that are always magnificent and for this I am grateful to the heron.

SUMMER ❦

Summer afternoon; to me those have always been the
two most beautiful words in the English language.

~ Henry James ~

EARTH

Most of us spend our lives at a distance from the very ground beneath our feet. We build barriers between it and us; floors, streets, sidewalks, patios, driveways and even lawns, all to keep the earth at bay, as if by touching this ground we become less than civilized. At least this is what we are taught; that we should avoid this dirt, that it is filled with disease or worse.

Yet those who work with the earth know something different. The farmers whose hands are etched from years of working the land or the gardeners who cannot wait for spring to feel the rich moist soil between their fingers can feel the life within it. There are still others who simply celebrate this dirt, who walk on it, dig in it and live with it for no other reason than to connect to an element of ourselves that is beyond basic, beyond ancient.

Dust to dust; the earth is where we came from and it is what we will become.

SUMMER LIGHT

The heat of the summer seems to drain the energy from the soil. The plants of spring wither and the dry earth cracks open while Indian Creek becomes a trickle. Yet not all living things retreat. Some wildflowers, such as Prairie Indigo and the Compass Plant, thrive in these conditions and once again the preserve changes into a different world.

Of course, there is also the light of summer. On some mornings the humid, saturated air hangs in the heat and sunbeams light the floating moisture like beacons in the woodland. Moments such as these are gifts and, like watching the northern lights or catching a glimpse of a fox, they are to be savored and treasured.

INSECTS & SPIDERS

In the humid days of late August, just above the patch of prairie that rests near the southern end of the preserve, the air is alive with thousands of bees, wasps, beetles, and dragonflies dancing across the tops of the prairie grasses. Others, such as the spider and praying mantis, wait patiently below for an unsuspecting few to venture within their grasp and present themselves as an appreciated meal.

At first, the sound created by this multitude of tiny creatures appears haphazard and chaotic. But after watching for several hours I begin to understand that there is a true balance to this world of bugs. It is a world where the hunters and the hunted, the victims and the survivors play out a timeless, unconscious ritual. There are no morals in this world, just a pragmatism where each creature has a role and, in the end, where life goes on.

45

If all mankind were to disappear, the world would regenerate back to the rich state of equilibrium that existed ten thousand years ago. If insects were to vanish, the environment would collapse into chaos.

~ E. O. Wilson ~

TIME

There are days I want to just stop. When I want to grip the present and pull the plug on time itself, but the hours race by. The distance between dawn and dusk seems measured in blinks and the day that carried a morning's promise is suddenly awash in a night sky.

Many people have found ways to stretch time and slow the hands of the clock. For me, it is simply by walking in the woods and watching. On these days I can actually see the minutes pass by as the shadows creep across the forest floor. I can follow an ant's trek over giant twigs, hear the stream's gentle murmur or just close my eyes and listen. It is here in the woodland that nature opens the space between the seconds and allows me to rediscover the true measure of a day.

HOPE

Hope exists in possibilities; in the potential of what may come to pass. Because we are conscious of our future, hope is also a uniquely human trait. And it is the future where hope resides, not in the past and certainly not in the fleeting present, but in the realm of what might be. So when a seed is lifted from the woodland floor by a gust of wind or dropped from an outstretched branch, it carries with it that potential of a future we will know and cherish. We endow that seed with our own hope, our own desire for the continued renewal of that cycle of nature.

But now we are entering an age of ambiguous direction. Changes to the environment occur daily. Temperatures rise and clean water becomes scarce. The cycles that once seemed as reliable as clockwork have been replaced by uncertainty. And while many of us work to mitigate these effects, we continue to struggle with our own imperfections. In the meantime, we watch the seeds that float through the summer air and we hope.

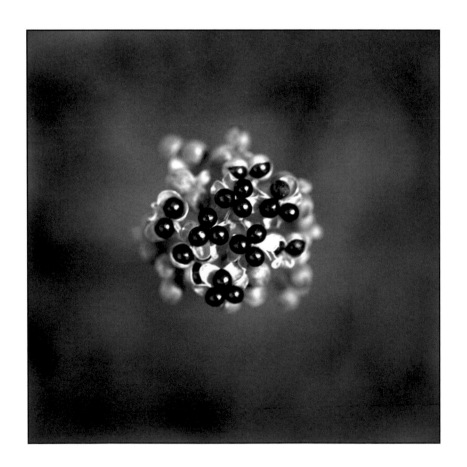

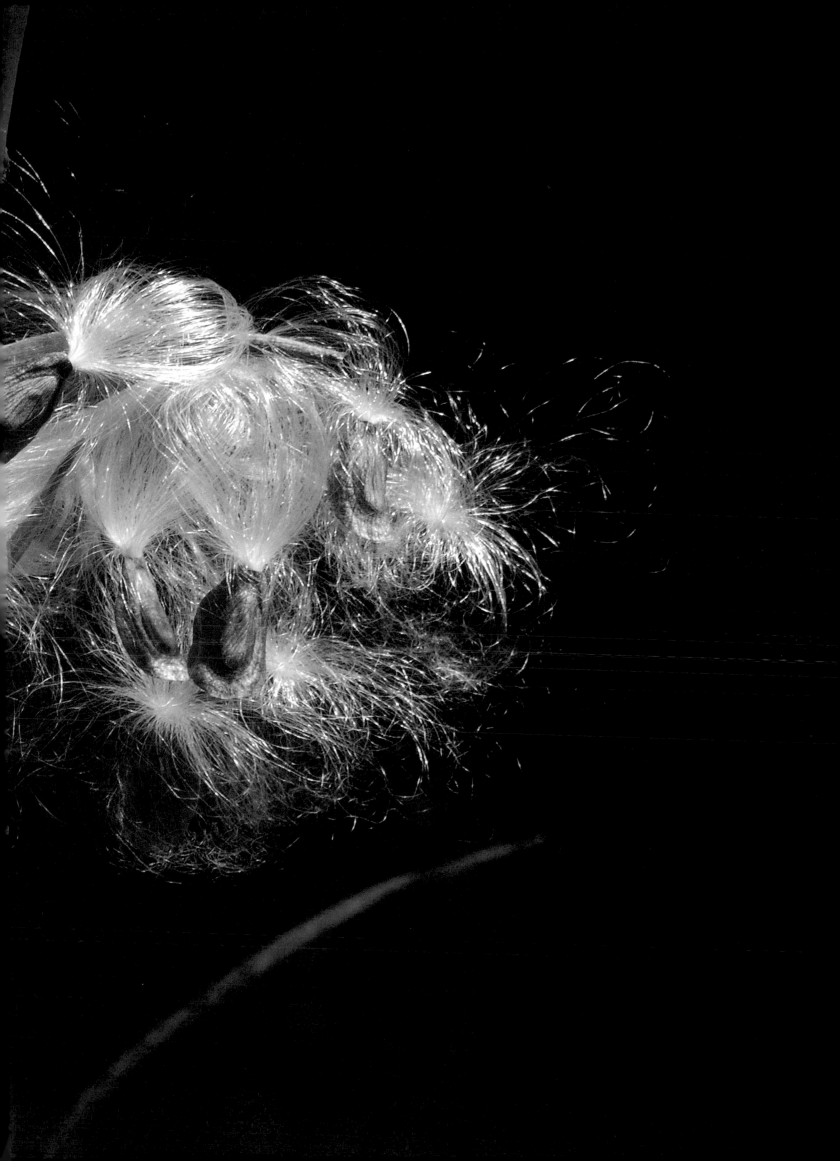

CURIOSITY

The need to know, to explore and to find an answer only to have that answer beg another thirty questions, this is what drives my life and what shakes me awake in the middle of the night. Curiosity is an enthralling and gnawing ache that rattles unending questions in my head. And so I search and walk through doorways for no other reason than to see what waits on the other side. This quest for understanding seems innate, as if there is a collective desire to untangle the riddles of our existence, even though, for me, there will always be more questions than answers.

THE CREEK

Although, in its simplest form, a creek can be defined as a small body of water traveling from a higher point to a lower point, a creek is anything but simple. Over its course, it provides a home for thousands of creatures, it replenishes the roots of countless plants and even resculpts the very land through which it travels.

The creek also has many faces. One day it reflects the sky as the sunlight sparkles across its surface. Then, on a hot, dry summer day the creek can be reduced to a trickle of tired, muddy water pushing across the parched ground. At other times, storms can send the creek over its banks, where it thrashes through the woodland.

There are also the warm spring days when I can stand near its bank and hear the voice of the creek. It is a voice that speaks in a rolling, burbling, ancient tongue that comforts and consoles me and tells me tales of all that I have forgotten.

AUTUMN ❦

Delicious autumn! My very soul is wedded to it, and if I were a bird I would fly about the earth seeking the successive autumns.

— George Eliot —

PERSPECTIVE

In 1956 I was five years old. In 1956 a grand White Oak on Guy Reed's property was 280 years old. At five years old, that same oak was already twelve feet tall and stretching towards the sky; Jacques Marquette was paddling his canoe up the Chicago River; the Algonquins had heard of the light-skinned fur traders and some had even seen them; the American Revolution was still 100 years away; and Johann Sebastian Bach was yet to be born.

So even though a tree does not consciously note the passing of time, nor does it record or even care about the events of human history, it was there. The same air that rushed through its branches fanned the flames of the Great Chicago Fire, the same rain clouds that soaked its roots washed the ground at Gettysburg in 1863, and the same sun that nourished the leaves of this great tree warmed the hands of the young boy who was to become my grandfather.

Now this same tree allows me to sit by its side, to rest in its shade, to write, to imagine and to remember.

CHANGE

Autumn sneaks up on me. I wilt in the late summer heat and only when the nights dip into the forties do I realize that fall is near. Within a few days of that first evening cool, I can look out our window and see the willow begin to shed its leaves as the first bits of yellow appear along the tops of the woodland oaks.

For about three weeks in late September and early October the leaves of fall offer an opportunity to truly celebrate the colors of nature. On late afternoons, the sun moves towards the horizon and lingers over the pond. The light then finds its way deep into the woods and the leaves that lay hidden in shadows during the day now burn with color as if ignited by the sun's last rays. Within a few minutes the colors fade to grey as twilight takes over the evening sky.

SOUND

Walking into the woods, the sounds of nature remain muffled with the noise of the day ringing in my ears. Another few minutes and the rumble of traffic begins to ebb. Soon I can hear the first crunch of my own footsteps along the bark-lined path and then the notes of the chickadee emerge along with the unmistakable scuffling of grey squirrels racing up and down the trunk of a nearby oak.

As the static continues to dissipate, I begin to hear the rustle of the leaves as an afternoon breeze brushes past. Only then can I take a deep breath and truly hear the essence of the forest.

MUSHROOMS

In the fall, the woodland canopy brightens with a seasonal show of color, but the forest floor seems spent. The last of the wildflowers has come and gone and the colors that remain come from the False Solomon Seal's red berries or the few brilliant leaves that lie among the browning foliage.

Then, one day, mushrooms begin to push their way through the dark humus, dotting the landscape. I am never quite prepared for this display, since to me mushrooms are beige and wrapped in cellophane, either whole or pre-sliced and sit on a grocer's shelf. But here in the woodland they are bright white and orange and yellow and red. Some are just a few centimeters high with tiny spines while others are giants, covering several feet of ground.

Within a few weeks they have spread their spores and as quickly as they appeared, they are gone, hopefully to return again next year.

I am...a mushroom on whom the dew of heaven drops now and then.

 - John Ford -

Texture & Form

The noon sun flattens the landscape of the woodland, deleting the shadows. Not until hours later does the angled light expose the detail of a boulder etched by Ice Age glaciers or the ridges of the Burr Oak's bark.

Across the pond, the tops of the trees appear as bristles of a fine brush and the shoreline absorbs the water's ripples. As I walk deeper into the preserve, new images appear; prairie grasses, heads weighted with seeds, swirl in the wind as leaves that cover the ground create an autumn carpet over dormant frogs. Moving even closer I see the veins of a dragonfly's wing, the pollen specked pistils of a tall purple liatris and the world turned upside-down through drops of dew suspended from a spider's web.

Finally, as my hand presses against a thick cushion of rich green moss, the barrier between observer and participant is broken. At that moment I feel as connected to the fabric of the woodland as the roots beneath my feet.

REFLECTION

When the air is still and the fish have gathered in the depths, the pond disappears into itself. Reflected images of waterlogged branches reach up from beneath the surface and the mirrored twins of limbs stretch across the sloping shore.

In each reflection there is a lighter and a darker side, offering a natural balance of opposites. These images can be reminders of our own struggle to define the balance within the yin and yang. But moods, like reflections, can be fleeting and in a moment the shadows are revealed for what they are and all it takes is a sudden breeze or a duck's wake to break the spell of doubt.

Leaves

The beauty of an ordinary object can sometime remain hidden simply because the commonplace is taken for granted. So as I began to wander in the woodland, the leaves that covered the ground or filled the trees were nice, but not much more.

Over the next year I began to examine the details of the preserve in a very different way, eventually seeing the intricate patterns on each individual leaf. Now, when I walk the paths of the woodland, I am transfixed by them, finding each one a work of art, each one unique.

As the seasons change so do the leaves. In spring the new foliage coats the preserve with a fresh luminescent green that can only be found at this time of year. In early winter the fallen ones form a grand mosaic on the forest floor as if a million-piece jigsaw puzzle had been spread across the landscape. In February clumps of dry red-brown leaves huddle on cold branches giving the otherwise barren woodland a splash of color. And in the fall, the layers of color change daily as the leaves cascade through the air and dazzle me with their brilliance.

Leaves may still be commonplace, but now I know that they are no longer ordinary.

Autumn is a second spring when every leaf's a flower.

- Albert Camus -

THE BORROWERS

The concept of owning land is odd. If anything, we, as transient beings, are borrowing the land. The Earth was here well before Homo sapiens emerged from the tangled web of evolution and it will be here well after we have passed through the membrane of existence.

But our consciousness truly is Eden's apple, for in the complex realm of our firing neurons there are many different paths that we can choose. So during my all too brief life on this earth I would like to walk the path taken by many others; to feel the soil beneath my feet, to revel in nature's ever-changing wonder, and to do what I can, within the course of human culture, to minimize the scars we all leave upon the face of our only home.

Though there are times I lose track of this goal, when I put aside the future and rationalize the present, only to be faced with the potentially devastating consequences of my own behavior. In the end, my hope is that the generations who follow will forgive us for our indiscretions and that they will have the knowledge and wisdom to survive the sins of their fathers.

WIND

In late autumn, after the leaves have browned and fallen and before the snows coat the ground, the wind pulls voices from the trees. These raspy whistling moans are clearest near dusk, as if the last rays of the sun had sent a blast of breath to loosen their bark-coated tongues. At first the trees seem to whisper, but then the branches sway and howl as if some cruel arborist joke is being passed from limb to limb until the entire forest is shaking with delight. For a moment the wind subsides and then once again it rushes forward, whipping the woods into a frenzy of whistles, creaks and groans.

This chaotic dance of branches and air sends a chill through my bones and tells me to run from some imagined menace of the night. Despite my fear, I choose to stay, for the voices of the trees call out and I want to listen.

WINTER

I prefer winter and fall, when you feel the bone structure of the landscape.
Something waits beneath it; the whole story doesn't show.

- Andrew Wyeth -

Exposure

The light of winter can be harsh. The dark browns of the bare forest stand in stark contrast against the bright snow. And without the canopy of leaves to diffuse the sunlight, the shadows of the trees stretch across the frozen ground like stripes on a zebra.

As barren as winter can be, this is my favorite season. The preserve opens up visually. Obstructions to seeing deep within the woods are gone and patterns within the once hidden landscape, now lie exposed.

As an observer, I tend to view the seasons of the woodland in relative terms. At first, the colors in winter appear dull and almost non-existent compared to the brilliance of summer. So it takes time to adjust my eyes to the vast array of deep greens emanating from moss covered tree trunks and rust toned orange of oak leaves still clinging to cold dormant branches.

And then there is the snow. At first glance the frozen landscape appears to be stark and colorless, but closer examination reveals a distinct soft-hued blue that seems to glow from within, as if the snow had captured the sky and buried it beneath a sea of white.

Morning Light

In that first hour after the sun washes the darkness from the night air, the light that spreads across the landscape contains a clarity and freshness that wanes as the shadows of the day grow shorter.

Yet even after a lifetime of sunrises, I'm still uncetain if this early light is truly different or whether it is the optimism of a new day that colors the morning sky.

Fog

Fog surrounds and envelops the landscape, limiting my ability to see, but in a positive way, for the fog also softens details so that objects such as trees or leaves take on a completely different look. A branch that may have been lost against a backdrop of the pond's shoreline suddenly becomes clear, standing out against this curtain of moisture.

Fog also creates a mood. It absorbs sounds and diffuses light, it mutes the air and instills a sense of tranquil intimacy that embraces me as the world outside disappears and the path that lies before me seems to be mine alone.

First Snow

A few white puffs of lazy, easy snow float slowly through the air, then touch the ground and instantly disappear. But there are enough of them for me to call out, "It's snowing!" as friends rush to witness autumn's last hurrah. The moment is magical, as if we had forgotten what snow was and now here it is, created again for the first time.

That night the flakes fall thick and heavy, stacking one on top of the other until any evidence of a once familiar landscape is coated with a cold, sparkling frosting. Morning brings the sun and the glistening woodland beckons. It is a new world and I alone blaze a trail through uncharted territory, leaving fresh footprints that mark my progress. This will be a good day.

MELANCHOLY

We humans are an odd lot. We tend to interpret the world around us with our emotions and then project those same emotions back onto the world. We see the events of nature as either heroic or evil. A brave sparrow protects her nest from an aggressive blue jay or a wicked coyote devours a family of defenseless ducklings. In reality, nature is neither kind nor cruel, beautiful nor ugly, it just is.

Even with this understanding, there are days when I find myself walking a woodland path only to be suddenly drained by a sense of melancholy that washes over me and colors the landscape. Sometimes this feeling comes about simply because of the remarkable quality of the day juxtaposed with the insanity of the world at large. At other times it can be brought on by some bit of nature that reminds me of the impermanence of my own journey and the tenuous hold I have on this thin band of life.

This sense deepens on days when gray light filters through the overcast sky and the air hangs over the woodland. At these moments I try to remember that the preserve itself is not despondent and that, like all things, this too shall pass.

ICE

The transformation of water into ice is a simple process, although the outcome is almost always extraordinary and complex. Bits of moisture cling to meadow grasses and build crystalline blocks in the frigid hours before dawn. The stream's winter flow washes against the banks lining the waterway with sheets of frozen waves. Quiet pools of water construct thin-layered surfaces that crack like a sugar glaze when pressed with the tip of my shoe.

The very structure of ice is fleeting. Under the rays of a December sun that rides along winter's horizon, the frozen landscape is constantly reshaped. Eventually the thaw of spring reduces these transient sculptures to pools of liquid until their inevitable return next year.

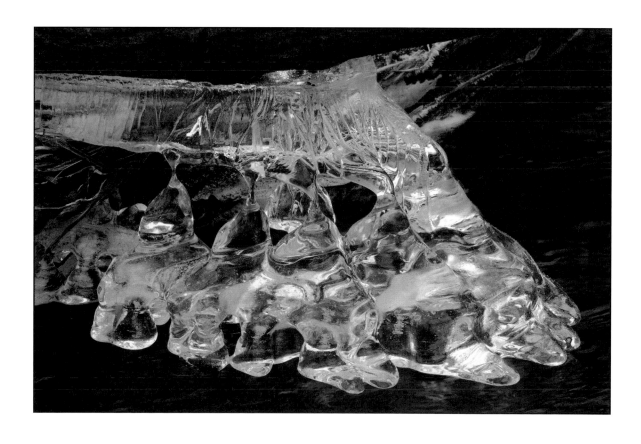

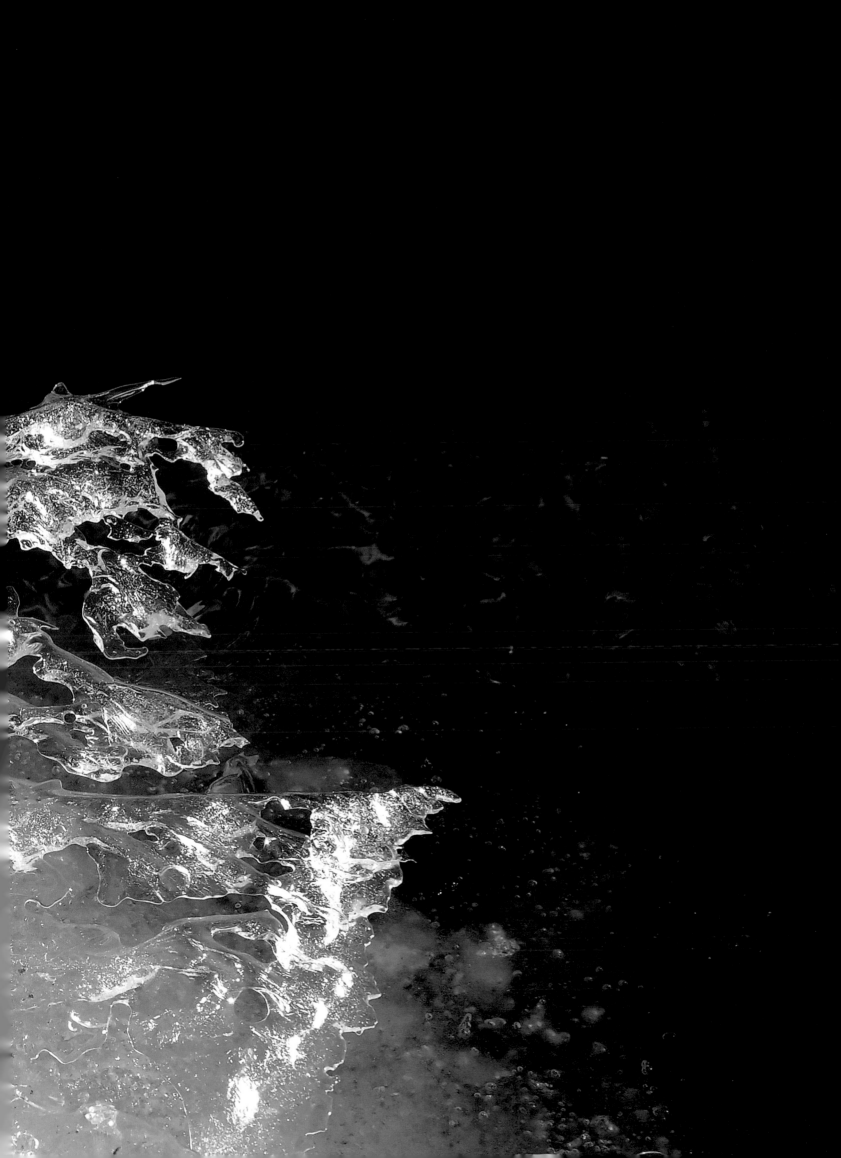

TREE

Every tree reaches a moment in time when life stops, but the transition from living to dead is not like it is for us. There is no pulse that ceases or final exhale. As observers, we might not even know of a tree's fate until the leaves of spring no longer offer a cover for the forest floor.

Even in death a tree emanates a sculptural sense of the aesthetic. Stark brittle branches still reach towards the sun's warmth. Bleached white wood peeks through gaps in gray bark while drying roots continue to grip the dark soil. There is a majestic triumph in a tree's decay.

In this regard I envy the tree. For years after death I would like to stand guard over my home, giving those who pass a glimpse of who I was while I continue to nuture the cycle of life.

January

A bright coating of fresh snow lies across the mid-winter meadow, disguising the paths that lead up the hillside and away into the woods. Six inches last night and another three expected tomorrow. The drifts are deep enough in parts to crest over the rim of my boots, tumbling bits of soft frozen powder down along my socks where it melts against the warmth of my feet.

Beneath the snow, the ground is as hard as bricks. Still, the seeming impossibility of spring readies itself just inches from the sole of my boot. Blackberries, Hepatica, and Bloodroot are just weeks away from pushing winter aside and covering the woodland floor with their annual display of nature's rebirth.

Pond Song

As autumn wanes, winter begins to grip the pond. Each night the ice battles against the open water, advancing across the surface with its crystalline blanket, but as daylight appears the sun and wind force the ice into a temporary retreat. Eventually cold triumphs and the creatures beneath the surface settle in for a long, dark sleep.

The days continue to shorten and the temperature drops and soon the ice thickens and the pond begins to sing. At an inch, a continuous symphony of tiny notes echoes across the lake as the frozen water expands into itself. At six inches the frequency slows as large sheets crack with the ping of a hundred foot piano string, racing across the length of the pond. Finally, at twelve inches, the sound evolves into an eerie boom that reverberates deep within the pond.

As I walk on the frozen surface I can hear and feel the occasional rumbling beneath my feet. It gives me an uneasy feeling, for despite my confidence in the strength of the ice, the sound makes it seem as though the pond itself were alive. That perhaps it is just waiting for some unsuspecting hiker to signal that it is feeding time for Reed Pond.

Evening Light

A setting sun designates the end of each day. Some days it eases past the horizon, leaving behind a vibrant array of color. Other times it slips away, hidden behind a layer of grey, indistinguishable clouds, as the daylight slowly fades into night.

But no matter how the sun marks the end of our day, it will never repeat itself, for no two sunsets will ever be the same. It is as if the sun's final light reminds us that our own day was unique and for proof it stamps the evening sky.

EPILOGUE & SUCH ⚜

Nature is beneficent. I praise her and all her works. She is silent and wise. She is cunning, but for good ends. She has brought me here and will also lead me away. She may scold me, but she will not hate her work. I trust her.

— Johann Wolfgang von Goethe —

Why This Book

Every book has a point of view expressing some value or theme the author hopes to communicate to the reader. Sometimes that moral is clear and concise while other times the reason for putting words on paper is vague, usually with the conscious intent of leaving the reader uncertain.

In writing this book I do not want to leave the reader with any possible sense of uncertainty: Every time thirty-six acres of meadow, woodland, prairie or forest is cleared to create another subdivision, another strip mall or to extend a highway, we are losing a Reed-Turner Woodland.

For me to state that we should just stop building new homes or offices would be naïve. Even so, it is clear that not enough consideration is given to land management and the conservation of open space in the planning of the ever-expanding realms of suburbia. The idea that thirty-six acres of beauty, tranquility and biological diversity are leveled to build another bank, pharmacy or supermarket when those amenities already exist a few hundred yards down the road, is not always carefully thought through prior to breaking ground.

Fortunately, there are a number of organizations actively purchasing and conserving large tracts of undeveloped land. Nationally and internationally, The Nature Conservancy owns and maintains millions of acres set aside for natural habitat and The Sierra Club has made huge strides in creating public awareness of open space issues. More localized efforts are also making a difference such as here in Lake County, Illinois, where the Lake County Forest Preserve District has purchased thousands of acres of meadow, forest and farmland through voter referenda and also in the Village of Long Grove where the conservation of open space has been a long-standing priority.

In the meantime, those who sigh a deep sigh each time another billboard appears declaring "New Development" can only hope that someday the incorporation of open space into our communities will be just as important as the creation of new homes and retail. Until then, I suggest buying a bicycle, planting your own vegetable garden and becoming involved with your local community government.

Anyway, just a thought.

Notes on the Photographs

All of the photographs in this book were taken using Nikon SLR equipment. A few were shot with an F100 using Fugi Velvia 100 film. Most images were taken with digital cameras including a D100, D300 and a D2x. The only post-photography work was accomplished using Adobe Photoshop for color and contrast correction along with some burning and/or dodging as would take place in any darkroom. It is always my intent to present images that are as faithful to the actual scene as possible.

A FEW THOUGHTS ON PHOTOGRAPHY

Photography is both much simpler and much more complex than it appears to be at first glance. Almost everyone has used a camera but few of us stop before taking a picture to really see what it is we are photographing. Anyone who wants to take more than a snapshot must not only take into account the basics of how to use a camera, but of much greater importance is an understanding and connection to your environment and truly seeing your subject. The art of taking a good photograph can be broken down into several specific areas.

LOOKING AROUND

Most of us, when we walk down a path in the woods, look straight ahead with an occasional glance down or to the side. A movement might catch our attention and we'll see a deer or squirrel darting through the brush. But what we don't usually do is stop on the path and examine the texture of the bark on the nearest tree or look straight up and see the way the light filters through the branches.

Becoming aware of your surroundings and taking in more than what is in your general line of sight is the first step in capturing a good image

OPEN TO SEEING

Every day that I grab my camera and head into the preserve, I know that out there somewhere is a really good photograph, waiting to be taken. I don't have a clue as to where it is or when I might find it, but I know that it is there. There are also days that I'm distracted, when something is on my mind or I'm tired or just a grump. On those days the scene that's waiting to be photographed may be right in front of me and I just don't see it.

Finding the photograph is a matter of being open and ready to see. I can take a hundred shots, but if I'm not "seeing" that day, I will have only taken a walk in the woods.

BATTLING THE MIND'S EYE

Our eyes are much like the lens of a camera. We focus, our pupils dilate or contract based on the amount of light and the size of the image remains consistent (unless we use a telephoto lens such as a pair of binoculars). Yet once the image from our eye reaches our brain, we become very selective in what we choose to see.

We can pick a person we know out of crowd of a hundred people in less than a second, because we focus on the familiar. If we then want to take a picture of our friend in that crowd, we will almost always point the camera in her direction and click the button. When that photo is developed, we'll look at it and wonder why the heck we took that picture until we realize that our friend was somewhere in that mass of people.

Our eye has picked out our friend and our mind has filled our mental frame with her, even though the reality of the image is that she is only a tiny piece of the whole.

It is the same in all photography. Our tendency is to see a specific object whether it is a person, a building, a tree or a flower. We point the camera in that direction and take a picture only to find out later that the object is only a dot in the final print.

When we take any photograph, understanding how the image or the object of our interest fits within the frame of the camera is critical to taking a good photo.

PERSPECTIVE
Our eyes are approximately in the middle of our heads. This means that, on average, our line of sight is around five feet four inches from the ground. So when we take a photograph, it is almost always from the level our eyes. Kneeling or sitting down can open up an entirely new range of observing and photographing. An object that may have appeared mundane from five feet four inches away, may suddenly become very interesting while seated on the ground only two feet away.

THE GIFT
Every now and then, while strolling along a path, an extraordinary scene will suddenly appear. It may be in the form of a beam of light passing through the branches to land upon a grazing deer, or it may be a Luna Moth just emerging from its cocoon. I look on these moments as gifts. They sometimes come on so quickly you are caught off guard. One time I came across a Hummingbird Moth and was so entranced by it that for a few moments I forgot that I had my camera with me. I was fortunate that the moth cooperated and posed for another minute.

The more one is out and available to nature, the more often one will come upon these gifts. And when these gifts are presented, don't hesitate to use an entire roll of film (or an equivalent number of digital images) on a single subject, for each shot will represent a unique perspective and the one you didn't take may have been your best.

PHOTOGRAPHING FROM ONE SPOT
Over the course of a day, a single location can take on a vast variety of moods, especially in the early morning or as the sun glides through the last hour of the day. Packing a few bites to eat, a thermos of coffee, along with some extra rolls of film in a day pack, and a portable chair, then finding a spot to wait, can be a perfect way to spend several hours and a great way to view the ever-changing face of nature. Staying in one spot will also allow shy wildlife to approach closer than if you were crunching along a path.

NO AGENDA
And lastly, photographing anything (and nature in particular) is best when there is no specific time frame. "Dentist appointment in a half an hour. Got to take some photos first." This will not work. The less distracted we are the more open we are to seeing what is there.

The universe is sacred.

You cannot improve it.

If you change it, you will ruin it.

If you try to hold it, you will lose it.

~ Lao Tsu ~

About Tobin Fraley 🌿

     Born in 1951, Tobin Fraley spent his first ten years in Seattle, Washington, growing up in and around his grandfather's amusement park. Endless free rides on the park's bumper cars have had a profound and somewhat curious effect on Fraley's personality. Since Seattle he has lived in Berkeley, California, New York City, Kansas City, Missouri and currently resides in Long Grove, Illinois, where he and his wife Rachel own Woodland Grove Gallery. He is the author of three books on the history of Carousels along with a holiday children's story titled, *A Humbug Christmas*. Fraley currently teaches photography at the Chicago Botanic Garden and the Morton Arboretum and would someday like to open a restaurant that serves amazing breakfasts, but he knows that this is a crazy idea.

About Tori Trauscht 🌿

     Tori Trauscht is a co-founder of the Indian Creek Watershed Project and has been involved in conservation efforts around Illinois for the past twenty years. She is currently engaged in promoting public awareness and support for the recently completed Indian Creek Watershed Plan. As administrator of over twelve grants to restore natural areas in the Indian Creek watershed, her projects have included restoring the sedge meadow and tributaries at the Reed-Turner Woodland Nature Preserve, and completing many other projects to improve stream corridors, lakeshores and wetland complexes along Indian Creek - www.indiancreekwp.org

Friends of the Reed-Turner Woodland 🌿

     The Reed-Turner Woodland Nature Preserve is not a stagnant 36 acres. As Tori Trauscht points out in the foreword of this book, there is great deal of ongoing work necessary to preserve and maintain the land. To help with this process The Friends of the Reed-Turner Woodland was formed to raise the much-needed funding for these projects. For more information or to lend a hand, please contact the Reed-Turner Woodland Trust (a charitable, not-for-profit corporation) at 847/438-4743.

Resources 🌿

     For more information on resources concerning land management, conservation and open spaces, locating small nature preserves around the country, purchasing photographs seen in this book, author contact information and suggested reading, go to www.36acres.com

II + II = IIII
is a
mathematical
absolute.

—————————

"I can be wrong"
is an axiom
of human
understanding.

—————————

If we approach
our lives with these
thoughts clearly
established in
our minds,
the world can
and will be
a better place
for everyone.

Map of the
Reed-Turner Woodlan
Nature Preserve

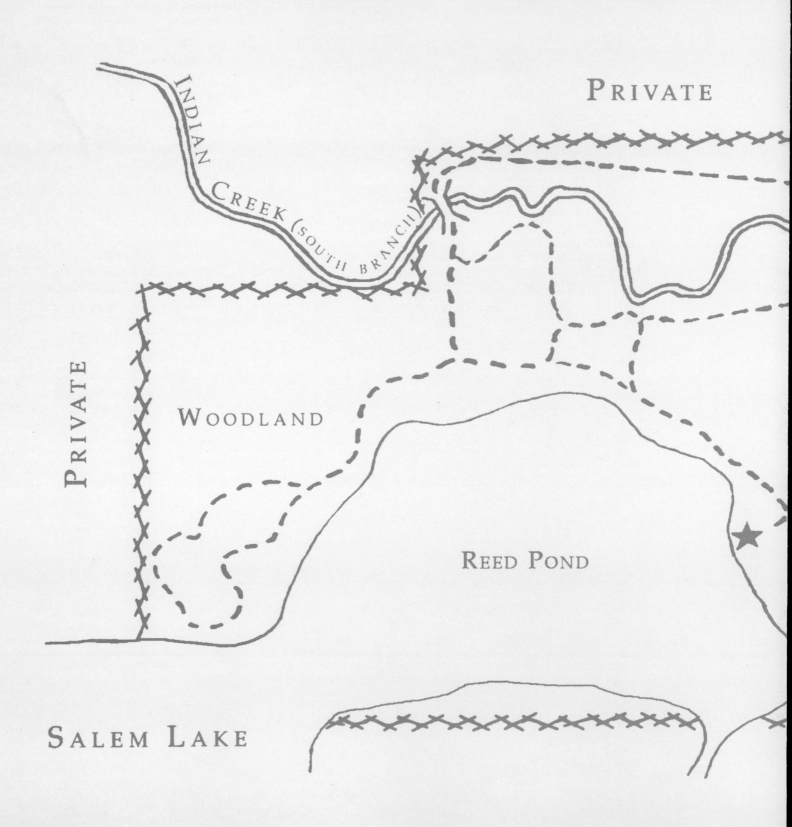

PRIVATE

INDIAN CREEK (SOUTH BRANCH)

PRIVATE

WOODLAND

REED POND

SALEM LAKE